THE POWER

OF POSITIVE

THINKING

For people who want to
learn how changing your
thinking can change your
world for the better

Have you ever fallen into a rut? Felt stressed and shut down? Or just completely overwhelmed? Desperately wanting a better life... Turning your life around? If so this is the most important message you will ever read Because when people are miserable and depressed. They become more miserable... more negative...more depressed... And life only gets worse! They grumble at their terrible situation... Curse fate... Blame others... And become MORE miserable. They never ask the following question: Why is it that some people are so lucky... Get everything they want... The good job... The good relationships... The good everything. While others are always so unlucky... Constantly stressed... Always anxious... Nothing seems to work - as they are constantly struggling through life. It all comes down to this little secret - The Power Of Positive Thinking.

CHAPTER 1

The Power of the Word and Positive Thinking

Positive thinking is a process by which we create thoughts that are focused and manifested by us to push forth energy out to become reality. When you think of a positive thought you do what is needed to make that thought become your reality; positivity benefits both the self and others in kind. In order to really understand positivity and its effects, we have to understand how the mind works. By getting a grasp on how the unconscious and conscious mind work, together in relation to ourselves, helps show us how to manifest positivity in our lives.

In order to conjure up positive energy within ourselves so we can radiate that positivity outwards, we have to look at how we use our energy as it is expressed through our thoughts mentally and emotionally and how we execute them physically in our lives. All these things involve learning how to maximize our potential of positivity. In essence, positivity is a mental attitude that is at the core of all our thoughts, including words and actions that enable our positive ideas to become reality.

When we have a positive mindset, we can expect no less than a favorable outcome in our lives. When we live in a positive state, we can expect no less than health, joy and a good result in things we want in life. Truth be told, whatever the mind expects is what it finds. Don't be fooled though, it takes work to be positive especially in a world such as ours today. But the more it is incorporated in our lives the easier it becomes. In fact, many people think the notion of incorporating positivity into their lives is just a bunch of crap and bull. This is because many people who are down, depressed or indeep trouble are told "Think Positive" by people who themselves really don't believe those words. All of our feelings, beliefs and knowledge come from our thoughts both consciously and subconsciously. They create our state of mind which manifests in the way we present ourselves to ourselves and the world in kind. When you say "life is the worst", "I wish I was dead" or anything negative, it shows in our behavior and how we move about in the world. It is us, no one else, who controls our minds and how we think. Conditioning is a reinforcement of our mindset. This is whether we are aware of this fact or not.

If we think there is no way out of a hole, whether we dug it or selves or not, we will never get out of the hole. With this said, we can either be negative or positive, enthusiastic or dull, active or passive. It's our choice no one else's. This is what happens when we hear stories where the odds are stacked against a person and they win. It's possible what makes their story different than yours. It's their mindset.

The biggest factor in whether we get what we want in our lives is how determined our attitude to change things is. It is our attitudes plus feedback from way back, starting with our parents, then friends and society which affect our "self" and how we see ourselves. These things help foster our self-image and how we project ourselves in the world as a result. The other thing that keeps us in a state of being unable to change our mindset is the constant inner conversations we have with ourselves that keep the wrong ideas about ourselves going. We have these conversations with ourselves both subconsciously and consciously like the thoughts that feed our state of consciousness, as well. The first step to positivity is to change the negative conversations we keep having with ourselves which become our attitude. The way this can be done is through what is called the **Three C's.**

The Three C's are:

1.   **Commitment** - Make a conscious commitment to be positive. This means committing yourself to positive things such as learning, family, friends, environment and positive causes. When you give others positive encouragement it feeds your own positivity.

2.   **Control** - Control "your" mind. Keep your mind focused on what is important in your life. You can foster this by setting goals and priorities for yourself and sticking to them. Learn to develop strategies to deal with problems. Be honest with yourself and learn to relax.

3.   **Challenge** - Have courage in yourself and be courageous in your life. Do your best and don't look back. Seek learning and view change as opportunities not set backs. Consider your options if they fit your goals and dreams. Don't let anyone or anything prevent you from what you want. Try new things. Keep conscious track of your mental and physical health. Be optimistic and do not surround yourself with negative people, things or situations.

Studies have shown that people with the three C's are winners in good times and survivors in the bad. Research has also shown that people who also begin to modify and change their internal conversations with themselves find almost an immediate improvement in their performance and situation. Their energy level changes also with this right away. It is commitment, control and courage that helps a person become their best selves for themselves and then in the world.

The other consideration is the idea of happiness versus inner peace. Are the two the same or are they two different things? Many people confuse the two. They are "**not**" the same. Case-in-point: One can have a miserable existence but still be at peace in their inner core. This is what gives them the strength to sustain their miserable existence but this does not create their happiness. You can be suffering at the loss of a loved one whether through death or a break up and still be at peace inside. Inner peace is what allows us to accept the dreadful with resignation to sustain it. Happiness is a transient fix to things that one gets from stuff, position and comfort. Peace on the other hand is a deeply felt internal quality that the material or physical can't define. Inner peace is that part of ourselves deep within us that says "It is so" when life seems to slap us and turn against us.

Another thing that affects our state of being is our view of good and bad. First of all, we don't all think of the same things as being good or bad. One person may find something horrible, yet another will like it. It's personal. So to help find our inner peace, we have to learn to let go of the good or bad notion and say "well it is what it is". You need bad experiences to know what good ones are. Life is about balance that creates harmony which ultimately gives us peace.

Living in a bad moment helps us to understand that we have illusions that we need to let go of to make peace and sense of that bad time. This doesn't mean we tolerate everything by any means. What it means is when we see what we consider bad we have to find what it taught us so we can learn from the experience, if we learned it at all, and then keep moving.

This is what is called letting go. The sum of all the total bad experiences we face in our lives, if we cultivate and keep clinging to them, can devastate you and keep you from moving on in your life, as well as ruining the life you have left. Our minds and bodies were not designed by nature to keep debilitating experiences and feelings stored in our bodies and minds for our whole existence.

This is what makes the difference from suffering in one's whole life and being or having a painful experience that you can move on from and still live your life.

Negativity is a form of resistance to that which is Positive. They are in fact polar opposites. Look at a battery. One end is negative and the other is positive. But you need both to get the battery to work for ionized charges to occur. You cannot have the good without the bad is the same idea as negativity and positivity. The difference is the choice you make to decide which charge you choose to be. The best way to let go of negative energy in and out of your life and self is to define where it stems from in the first place.

Negativity can range from irritability, agitation and impatience to fierce anger, hatred and total despair. You have to get to the source of what triggers the negativity in your life to get rid of it. This can be hard because some negativity is triggered by things we cannot control like certain body pain and people who refuse to go away. This is where mind-over-matter comes in. Once the source is identified whether physical, emotional, mental, or spiritual and you decide not to let it go, you are choosing to keep negativity in your life. This means you do not want a positive change. Easier said than done, it is of course, a process, but to do so is self-sabotage.

The first step on the road to positivity is to stay in the now. Surrender to the moment by accepting and staying in the present. We cannot change the past, but we can change how we go into the future.

CHAPTER 2

The Power of Thoughts and the Mind

The average person, as our selves, processes up to 60,000 separate thoughts a day; 90% of those are subconscious thoughts. Subconscious thoughts are automatic ones that are produced by our minds on a subconscious level and continue to be produced without any conscious effort or input from our conscious mind. This means we think about things all day and night long without consciously trying to do so. If you were to think of our mind as a little minicomputer these are automatic computer programs that automatically respond to stimuli in our environments. In this regard, depending on our environments, our life conditions and histories that are stored in our minds, the way our mind is set, determines the condition of the thoughts we have, even subconsciously. For example, we may smile and say we are happy, but deep down we are sad because of a horrible childhood.

It is the subconscious mind that either stimulates the positive or negative thought patterns that guide us through our lives. With this in mind, if you are pre-programmed subconsciously to be negative then you will function as such. Subconscious negativity can prevent one from evolving, reaching one's goals and constantly bombarding an individual with the idea of road blocks and limitations. These are called success blockers. This is because they prevent you from getting where you want to go in your life.

It is automatic thoughts that prevent you from being successful. They determine your patterns, behaviors and attitudes starting deep in the subconscious and then permeating our conscious state of being.

What happens with subconscious thoughts, actions and behaviors is they get validation from the stimulation in your environment. It is the environment that validates our thoughts from our subconscious and reinforces the negative mindset. A key factor is that it has been scientifically observed that one's "automatic thoughts" are actually triggered by common belief patterns called "schema" within a group of people who share the same challenges and or limitations in their lives.

So, in retrospect, although it is a process to change one's mindset, the first battle in regaining a positive mindset is to eliminate the thoughts that create the negative mindset in the first place. This is done by determining consciously those things whether thoughts or patterns that actually are triggered that block our positive selves on a day-in day-out basis. These are those limiting ay negative thoughts, attitudes and behaviors that when we think about we can start to control. This is because we see how they manifest in us and then become a part of our daily thoughts and behaviors. If you don't pinpoint the sources of negativity you cannot change them. It's that simple.

Once identified, the next step in regaining our positive mindsets back is to consciously and actively change those thoughts we have that keep us blocked and in a negative mindset. Changing the negative mindset patterns is called cognitive modification. We change how we think from the subconscious level up. In this case, we replace negative thought patterns consciously with those cognitive patterns that have been shown to give us positive responses instead. The way this is done is by reconditioning the old thought patterns we have and replacing them with new ones. If we use the computer analogy, again, we are replacing an old worn out program with a new, better one that functions at optimum speed.

This is not an easy process and in does not occur over night. But by incorporating positive thoughts on a regular basis as you feel the negative ones creeping in you start to change your mindset. The power of our minds is the second strongest thing we have; the first is the power of our spirits which is our wills despite the odds. It is our thoughts that are responsible to everything that happens to us in our daily lives. This means you have to be careful about what you think about. Thoughts and the mind is like a DVD and a DVD player. The DVD player is the mind and the thoughts are the DVD we put in it. In essence, what you play on that DVD is what you see and experience. What you think is what you live. If you think hopelessness you will live hopelessness and spread the hopelessness to those who live with you, thus the example of schema ensues. To change negativity you have to eject the Negative DVD and replace it with a Positive one. Thoughts are a creative process, as are the power of thought. It is indeed possible to train and strengthen our minds. What also happens is when thoughts manifest on the material plane, as in our lives, they also influence those thoughts of others around us.

So if you surround yourself with negative thinking people, you in turn will have a negative mindset. Negativity and Positivity are contagious. The mind is a fertile ground and thoughts are seeds. If you plant a seed and nurture it, it grows. If you nurture it with positive water you get a positive plant. If you water it with negativity a negative plant will grow. Thoughts manifest by the attention we give them, be it good or bad. So to manifest positive thoughts, we have to give them the positive attention they need to become manifested.

Thoughts pass through our subconscious first which in turn results in actions that correspond to the thought. Our thoughts also influence how others around us think because they are passed on to other people. A good example is when we ask someone to help us we do not know and they do so. They may say, I do not know why I am helping you, but help anyway. This is a manifestation of the positive. The Universe we live in is a cosmic mystery. Science tries to come up with logical explanations and sometimes they hit and sometimes they miss. The fact is, we are all part of the power of the Universe. The power of the mind is one of the creative aspects that the Universe has bestowed upon mankind. Our thoughts also work with the great force of the universal mind and its power.

The creating of positive thought is called "practical daydreaming." Practical daydreaming puts us in a positive scenario and sees us getting that positive thing we want in our lives time and again. It sets the tone in our subconscious to program us for us to obtain what we want. This is how someone, who against all odds in their lives accomplishes something others said, is impossible. The more things one adds to the practical daydream such as colors, sounds, scents and feelings the more real it becomes. It's important to use practical daydreaming when re-programming our mindset from negative to positive. The more we repeat the positive scenarios in our minds eye, the faster the subconscious begins to take them in as part of our experience. The subconscious doesn't differentiate between reality and imagination. Everything is real in our subconscious. Case-in-point: We all experience times when we know something is about to happen and then it does and we say "I knew that was going to happen". This is how the subconscious helps guide thought to manifestation.

The more you visualize positivity and you in the scene, the more it begins to manifest in your life. In this regard, it comes to light and becomes reality in a natural way. It's like putting new software in a computer, and as you use it you see more and more of the benefits it has.

I don't want to make you think this is all a peaches and cream experience. Incorporating positivity at the subconscious level does not occur over night and it takes work to make it as such. As much time you put into being positive and incorporating it in your mind is as fast as you will see the effects of positivity in your life. The process of incorporating positivity and using practical daydreaming can be used for changing or improving any habit ability or skill. You can use it to change your circumstances, and don't be fooled, people who are successful, use it all the time.

CHAPTER 3

Things You Can Do to Change Your Negative Mindset

As we have seen in the last chapter, the power of thought is a creative process. What we think passes into our conscious living patterns. So, if we are negative, it creates a negative setting for the negativity to thrive in. The automatic negative thoughts we have are triggered by deep rooted thought patterns and beliefs that are reinforced with people who in kind have the same thoughts and mindsets on the conscious level.

On the other hand, people who are considered positive and successful in their lives, all attribute it to their distinct positive set of cognitive patterns as positive thoughts in their belief systems. Negativity works the same way and, unfortunately, some people thrive on being negative. In order to execute a positive mindset, then you have to recognize your mindset and change it to positivity.

Here are some success enabling, and mindset enabling patterns:

1. **Believing in your Unique Skills, Talents and Capabilities**

Believing in our own innate skills, talents and capabilities is not only important from a professional development perspective. It also enables you to align your uniqueness in its entirety with your potential. Several studies reveal that we are the happiest and most effective when we can utilize our individual abilities to the highest degree possible. The objective is to allow you to rise beyond your current limitations and maximize your personal potential.

2. Viewing Life as a "Platform" for Opportunities

Viewing life as a big platform of opportunities opens doors for opportunities to materialize. It focuses our minds on the possibilities rather than the limitations. Have you ever wondered why some people seem to have a disproportionate amount of luck? They seem to be at the right place at the right time or meet the right people at the right time. The truth is that it isn't mere luck; most of these people look for opportunities and find them, because their mind is open and receptive to opportunities.

3. Accepting and Expecting Positive Change

Change has a tendency to reward people who embrace it. Welcoming change also means having the courage to explore new areas of potential success. An open attitude toward change is essential for positive change to take place.

4. Feeling Empowered and in Charge

Accepting responsibility for your own destiny and feeling empowered to shape your destiny according to your ideas is a key success factor. Successful people don't look for other people or circumstances to shape their destiny. They actively take control and create their destiny.

5. Persistence

Many people have great goals and visions. Unfortunately, the majority of people lose interest when the desired results don't materialize as quickly or easily as they anticipated - they give up and never try again. If you talk to people who have achieved great things in life, they will tell you that persistence is one of the key factors for their success. If you want to succeed, you need to be persistent.

6. Creating Mutually Beneficial Relationships

Creating mutually beneficial relationships with other people is not only important for our social well-being, but also for any kind of success we seek to achieve. It is by giving and taking that we open these doors to new, and sometimes unexpected, great opportunities.

7. Self Confidence and Self Esteem

A healthy level of self-confidence and self-esteem is not only necessary, it is essential for any kind of success we seek achieve. Only when you're comfortable with who you are and confident in what you can do, will other people believe in you and your abilities. This applies both to your personal life as well as your professional life.

8. Living with Purpose

All successful and generally happy people display high levels of purpose and action orientation. They keep their goals in mind, act on their ideas, follow through with their plans and stay the course until they achieve what they want.

9. Accepting and Offering Help

Many people have a hard time asking others for help. They confuse accepting help from others with weakness. This couldn't be farther from reality. Most successful people know about the importance of seeking and accepting help. They achieve their goals by leveraging other people's skills, strengths or contacts that they themselves lack. At the same time, they offer their help to others and extend their circle of valuable relationships.

10. Seeing Setbacks as Opportunities for Progression

Most successful people will tell you that they have had their share of setbacks. What sets them apart is that they accept setbacks as a natural phenomenon and have the ability to stay focused on their long-term goals. Setbacks are often accompanied by opportunities and it is key that you continue to look for these opportunities while you experience setbacks.

So these are some of the positive enablers to incorporate in your mindset to help change those negative thoughts and ideas into positive ones. On the other hand, these are the negative mindset enablers, once you identify what you want to rid your thought patterns of, as soon as you can pinpoint them.

The negative enablers are:

1.   **Feeling "not good enough"** - One of the key reasons why most people never reach their full potential is rooted in various forms of mostly unconscious beliefs of not being good enough. Although most people don't like to admit it, it continues to lead the charts of top "success blockers".

2.   **Fear and Resistance to Change** - Resisting change is mostly coupled with fear of the unknown. It is often evidenced by people who despite their unhappiness with their situation experience resistance to exploring opportunities for change. This resistance to change often leads to missed opportunities for advancement.

3.   Dependencies or Co-dependencies - Perceptions of dependencies and co-dependencies come in many forms. The result, however, is mostly the erroneous belief that our happiness and success is dependent on certain people, actions or circumstances outside of our control.

4.   Blaming Others for Missed Opportunities - We've all experienced instances where we thought other people stood in the way of our success. If these experiences turn into core beliefs that we carry with us, consciously or unconsciously, we not only create excuses for not progressing, but also obstacles to recognize ways to work around them and achieve our goals.

5.   Negative Expectations - There are multiple roots causing attitudes of negative expectations. Negative expectations in life tend to create self-fulfilling prophesies. If our mindset reflects an attitude of "I can't possibly do or achieve that", chances are that these predictions will become a reality. People with generally negative expectations often feel that life is a constant struggle and the next negative event is just around the corner. Imagine an athlete going into the Olympic Games thinking "I can't possibly win", or a CEO of a company thinking "I don't believe we'll ever succeed here". Releasing negative expectations is key to any form of success you may want to achieve.

6.   "I-Don't-Deserve" Attitudes - I-don't-deserve attitudes are often deeply rooted beliefs connected with beliefs of inferiority. Because we unconsciously believe that we don't deserve to strive for or achieve certain things, we either "go into the game" with low expectations for success, or often don't even try. The result is often that we simply miss out.

7.   Being a Victim of Circumstances - Victims of circumstances tend to accept unhappiness, mediocrity or failure as part of their destiny. Victims of circumstances often feel helpless, they think cannot or don't know how to do or achieve certain things. They often miss to realize that they have the power to change their circumstances. Therefore, they don't empower themselves to take control in shaping their circumstances according to their wishes.

8.   Procrastination and Passivity - Positive change always requires an orientation toward action. The best objectives and plans don't mean much if there's lack of action and follow-through. And yet, one of the top reasons most people don't progress or fail to achieve their goals is because they don't follow through.

9. **Earning Approval or Love of Others** - Cognitive patterns reflecting the necessity to earn the approval or love of other people can create serious limitations on many fronts. These attitudes divert our thoughts, behaviors and actions from our own individual needs and goals to doing to what's good for someone else. We can be supportive and helpful to others while staying true to ourselves.

10. **Rational Excuses for Irrational Behavior** - Rational excuses for irrational behavior come to light when we find "good reasons" for why certain things can't be done, or why we do things that shouldn't be done. Excuses, even if packaged in rational sounding reasons, can't hide the fact that we're still looking at excuses. As long as we believe these "good excuses" positive change cannot be initiated.

These things listed above are negative things we incorporate into our mind settings to block us from success. The idea is when you notice them cropping up to address them so you can start to change your automatic thoughts into positive ones. It's about training your mind to be positive. Like learning anything new, at first it is hard, but as you go along it becomes easier to do and then automatic.

Positive thinking is a mental attitude that is at the core of one's mind, thoughts, words, images and then behavior and conduct that promote growth, expansion and ultimately success with one is trying to achieve in one's life. A positive mind is one that expects no less than happiness, joy, health and a successful outcome in every situation in one's life. It is true that what the mind expects it finds. It is also a fact that not everyone is open or believes the idea of positive thinking. Some scoff at it while others find it to be nonsense. This is especially true when one has great odds and hardships stacked against them day in and day out. We have all either been told or told someone at some point in our lives to "Think Positive". However, most people do not take these two words seriously at all much less literally. This is because most of us do not really know what they mean. Both positivity and negativity are contagious. We all affect each other in this way when we meet people who either we allow in our lives or choose to keep them out. When we meet someone we decide how we want to deal with them based on things like their body language and then what and how they may say something to us. People sense our auras just as we sense theirs and just as they affect us we affect them as well.   It is also a fact that if we are positive people are more willing to help us when a problem arises. The same is true for most people will avoid someone they view as positive.

When we are in a negative mindset negative thoughts manifest in negative words, attitudes; causing more negativity in terms of moods and actions which are passed on to those around you as well. In order to turn the mind towards the positive, takes both inner work and training on our parts to de-condition those negative things that have become part of us. Negative thoughts and patterns do not change overnight. It took a long time for you to get to the point you are at when you are negative so it won't magically disappear.

One of the ways to begin to change a negative mindset is when a negative thought enters your mind to consciously replace it with a good one. It will try to enter again and then has to be replaced again. As often as it enters your mind that's how frequently it needs to be changed. It's almost like seeing two pictures in front of you a good one and bad one and you must consciously choose the good one again and again until it becomes automatic. It is persistence that teaches you to ignore the bad thoughts and replace them with positive ones. This does not however mean to block out reality and live in a fantasy. This means that if you have a problem instead of just feeling helpless and hopeless about it you look for constructive ways to resolve, alleviate or ease the problem in a positive way that benefits you for the better.

If you are faced with tough or difficult circumstances that can paralyze positivity fight to think in the positive here and now and try and not worry about tomorrow. Get through each moment to moment and find a sense of peace that you accomplished that. Keep focused on any glimmer of good that may be conjured up from your bad situation and use that as an incentive. In this case persistence goes a long way.

Another way to help you on your journey to positivity is to use repetition of positive affirmations when a negative thought comes up. When you feel the old negative thought creeping in replace it with a positive saying. For instance; I will not give in to this negative moment and I will succeed today. Negativity is like an addiction that constantly has to be battled by any positive means necessary.

CHAPTER 4

Make a Conscious Effort to Incorporate Positivity Through the Law of Attraction

For many of us being positive is almost an impossibility; especially in today's world. We are faced with things like unemployment, homelessness, illness just to name a few. And, if you are living one of these things you say "Are you crazy???" How can I be positive in my situation? It's not easy but it can help to get you out of your situation believe it or not.

When one is worried, living in fear and stressed one cannot think of solutions. One accepts the gravity of their situation without a positive fight to change it. In this case, fighting the odds is positivity. When you are in a negative mindset you are accepting a negative life and are saying "it's okay I am a failure". When you are negative you are embracing all that comes with it as well.

We have all heard of the law of attraction. Well, what does that actually mean? In the history of science it is a catch phrase for a term of laws that science applied to it stating that like things attract each other. In 391 BC Plato built on the Greek philosophers before him on ideas of phila/attractive force and *neikos*/repulsive force by postulating the first law of attraction which is "likes tend towards likes". He used examples of water to water and earth to earth at that time. A little later in 1250 AD, Albert Magnus elaborated on this idea and applied affinity to chemical systems and postulated the law of affinity.

So based on ancient philosophy and science, the law of attraction is taken and applied to all aspects of our lives. Since like attracts like, if you are positive, you will attract positive in kind. It's that simple. Likewise, we can attract negativity if we emanate those characteristics and can repel positivity which is called the law of repulsion. Now, to take the law of attraction and apply it to one's life means to bring something into existence by attracting it to you.

The law of attraction in this case says we bring things into manifestation based on our thoughts and beliefs to make it happen. For example, we may be inspired to take a particular action but the thought or belief in that action always comes first. An example of this would be let's say you never finished college and one morning you get up and the idea about going back comes into your head. The thought may stay with you for a while; could stay for days, weeks, months or even a year but it's in your head. Once that idea in your head keeps popping up, you start to examine the possibilities and find it is a do able thing. So now the thought is becoming a belief that you can do the action. Once the thought is backed up by the belief, it's up to you to take the step. In this case, it would be to go to the college you were thinking about and taking the proper steps to go back. So the law of attraction is a thought that turns into a belief that turns into an action to manifest your goal. You do not achieve anything in life if it is not a thought first. The second part is belief. You have to believe in the thought in order to carry it out. If you don't believe that something is possible you will not follow through. It is that simple. The third is using the law of attraction to carry out the action that the thought first suggested. In essence it is a three part process. You thought something; you believed in it and attracted the actuality of action. In reality if you want positivity in your life you have to think it, believe in it and act positive to manifest what you want.

If you maintain a negative mindset or attitude it says you cannot succeed or get beyond what is creating the negativity or problems in your life. Positivity is a powerful weapon to fight and get what you want despite the odds that may be stacked against you.

A positive attitude can manifest in many ways.

Here are some ways you can start to change a negative mindset to a positive one:

1. Positive Thinking

2. Constructive Thinking

3. Creative Thinking

4. Expect to succeed

5. Face the problem with optimism that you will overcome it

6. Staying motivated to accomplish your goals you have set for yourself

7. Being inspired and inspiring others in kind

8. Not giving up

9. Choosing happiness

10. Believing in yourself and your abilities

11. Looking at failure and problems as a blessing in disguise

12. Always looking and seeking solutions

13. Seeing and Seeking opportunities

If you can incorporate positivity in your life, the benefits include:

1. Achieving goals and success in things you want out of life for yourself

2. Succeeding easier and faster

3. More happiness in general

4. More energy

5. Greater inner power and strength

6. The ability to inspire and motivate others by example

7. Experiencing fewer difficulties along the way

8. The ability to surmount any difficulty

9. Seeing life smile at you

10. Respect from others

These are the attitude traits you need to incorporate for positivity:

1. Consciously choosing happiness

2. Looking at the brighter side of things

3. Consciously choose to be and stay optimistic

4. Finding reasons to smile more often

5. Have faith in yourself and the Universe

6. Think about the futility of negative thinking and worries when they arise

7. Associate yourself with happy people

8. Read stories of inspiration

9. Learn to master your thoughts

10. Learn concentration and meditation

If you can instill these things in your life, you are on the way to attracting positive things to you, because you give off the same positivity. You will become a positivity magnet and a negativity repeller.

CHAPTER 5

Positivity When Abused

Suppose you may currently be in an abusive situation or have once been the victim of abuse. How does positivity fit in a person's life who has been damaged by hurt upon hurt for no apparent reason other than being alive? It is a fact that the emotional scars of abuse do last for years. The best thing an abused person can do is to try the best way to heal themselves through shedding all the negative programming shoved into them to accept the abuse. This way they can begin to heal. Many times years of abuse strips a human being of their sense of self and of their esteem.

The abused may even take responsibility and say it's their fault for the abuse which is what the abuser wants and is ridiculous to say the least. It is this very thinking that allows the victim to stay caught in the abuser's web. It allows the negative thoughts to take hold and stay with the victim sometimes their whole lives if it's not addressed. The first thing a victim of abuse has to do in order to heal and move on into a positive direction is to learn to face their past; accept the reality that it happened and then point themselves in a positive direction from that point in their lives. The victim must understand that no abuse is their fault and no one deserves to be abused period.

One way to start to turn away, in a positive fashion-form of abuse, is to look at the abusive situation differently. Would you allow someone you love or your best friend to take responsibility for being abused or allow the abuse to be done to them at all if you knew about it? Of course you wouldn't. You would make it known to them that they are a person of worth and do not deserve abuse under any circumstances.

Being a victim of abuse who reaches towards positivity is like someone climbing out of darkness. Have you ever felt your eyes blur and tear when you stay in a dark room too long and then go outside into a sunny day? You have trouble seeing at first and may cover your eyes from the sun rays. Then, while standing there, you gradually remove your hands that shade the eye and your eyes open fully and you are standing with your eyes wide opened in the sun. Well, this is the same way an abused person reacts to healing and positivity. They may reject it first or not know how to respond first but then get the idea and embrace it If you are a victim of abuse, you may not be able to control the thoughts and actions of those around you but you can control your own responses to them. The first thing you have to do is to declare that you are a survivor and then lift yourself up to a higher level.

No one can keep you down unless you allow them to. It is easier said than done, especially if you fear for your life or the life of a loved one but it can be done. Abusers count on fear and immobilized beings to kick. If you have been able to break free of abuse even by running away (because you fear for your safety) or getting help from authorities you are one step closer to regaining yourself back.

You may also be long rid of your abusers, but it still takes time to heal emotional scars. Everyone heals at a different speed -- there is no right or wrong way. A person that was abused must first and far most remind themselves that others have made it through and so will they. Also keep in mind many abused people who recover become better people for the experience believe it or not. You must remind yourself to focus on the positives in yourself (even the fact you survived the abuse) and leave the negative thought patterns behind as you do.

Just as with programming positivity in the mind for all of us the abused person must also do so. In doing so, they must let go of the painful past and its conditioning as well to free themselves to start over. As the victim does so, they are regaining control over their lives.

The next important thing is for them to have faith in themselves and their strengths. It takes a strong person to over-come abuse on any level. As you focus on rising above the abuse you endured, you start to meet the positive goals you set for yourself.

Here are some things a victim can do to let positivity into their lives:

1. Avoid negative people and situations like the plague; if it doesn't feel right stay clear.

2. Stop dwelling in the past (easier said than done) by looking forward to a better future. Do this by setting new positive goals for yourself.

3. When the negative thoughts creep in replace them with positive ones and remind yourself of them when you have to.

4. Surround yourself with positive people.

5. Try and find humor in things.

6. Join a group or an activity that is positive.

7. **Do Not** Allow Yourself to Be Labeled.

8. Learn to accept compliments.

9. Talk to a counselor, get into a support group.

10. Read and do things on building self-esteem.

To rid your life of abuse it's about overcoming those negative patterns that enabled the abuse in the first place. Over-coming abuse is a complex process. It can be very difficult and painful for the victim of abuse to handle the healing involved. Many times this is due to the overtly negative, critical and psychologically damaging thoughts that the abuser plants in their victims minds to control them. There is no quick fix to heal a victim of abuse; it's a process and takes work to bring positivity and light back to someone who has been in darkness and pain for sometimes years on end or their whole lives.

Self-esteem is the main thing to rebuild in order to reinstate positivity in a person of abuse's life. It is self-esteem that virtually affects every aspect of our lives. How we feel and see ourselves affects our choices, our abilities to give and receive love and gives us the fortitude to change things when they need to be changed. So in order for positivity to set into a person who was a victim of any abuse they must incorporate positive mental exercises into the healing process. Abusers thrive on criticism and destroying the victims self-esteem. So the abused has to fight to regain this back.

Because of the constant degradation involved in abuse, the victim becomes critical of themselves as well; so, some of the negative patterns that have to be changed, have to do with self-criticism

Ways to combat self-criticism is through:

1. First notice how often you are self-critical. When you are self-critical you are basically doing the same thing the abuser did to you. You are in essence re-abusing yourself and lowering your own worth and esteem.

2. Catch yourself when you are in a self-critical or negative thought about yourself. Ask yourself "Who's voice am I hearing when I say this about myself?

3. Focus on your positive aspects instead of dwelling on your faults. No one is perfect. Self-criticism can be damaging enough, but if you never give yourself credit for what you do have that's positive then you are in a devastating mode.

So, if you can do the first three things; you can now also include some self-esteem building in the mix.

Here are some things to focus on:

1. Set realistic and reachable goals. Both abusers and victims set unrealistic impossible high standards for themselves which is why the victim fails. In order to feel successful which is vital to one's self esteem set doable small goals that you can succeed in.

2. Stop comparing yourself to others. This sets you up to feel less than adequate and the person you are comparing yourself to as better.

3. Begin to nurture yourself. Disappointment comes when those who we think are supposed to nurture us don't. So do it yourself for yourself. No one can make up for the sense of deprivation someone feels or experienced and you can't expect someone to do it for you.

These are some simple things you can do to help change a negative mindset into a positive one. Like I said, it is not easy and it takes time. Go easy on yourself and incorporate these little things until they become automatic. You will notice that you are taking your life back when you do these things without having to make an effort. You are bringing positivity to yourself which is your deserved right.

CHAPTER 6

How Positivity Affects One's State Of Health

Being positive affects how we feel both emotionally and physically. As the earlier chapters point out positivity is a state of being. So with that said if we are in a positive mode it is bound to affect our physical bodies in a positive matter as well. Stress and anxiety lead the way to a negative state of mind which opens the door to all sorts of health problems. It is a fact that the human body responds to how we think feel and act.

When we feel stressed or upset our bodies respond by telling us something is wrong. This is called the mind/body connection. Sadness also can cause physical symptoms that go along with that state of being. An example would be feeling sick when we get bad news or our blood pressure rises when we get upset. Our bodies respond to our state of mind in those cases for the worse. Here are some physical symptoms that if one experiences on a regular basis may be telling us our mindset is out of whack (this does not discount the possibility that there could indeed be a physical problem):

1. Back Pain

2. Change in appetite

3. Chest Pain

4. Constipation or Diarrhea

5. Dry Mouth

6 Extreme Tiredness

7 General Aches and Pains

8 Headaches

9 Insomnia or Trouble Sleeping

10 Lightheadedness

11 Palpitations(feeling like your heart is racing)

12 Sexual Problems

13 Shortness of breath

14 Stiff neck

15 Sweating

16 Upset Stomach

17 Weight Gain or Loss

Of course, if you have any of these problems on an ongoing basis, you should consult your doctor to make sure there is no serious illness behind the symptoms. Once it is established you are relatively healthy, then you can start to look at your state of mind and if you are in a negative frame of mind. A negative frame of mind can create poor emotional health with physical symptoms as well. It can weaken your immune system, notice that when someone is under stress they are more prone to getting colds, infections or sick. When someone is under stressful conditions they do not tend to take care of themselves as well as they should.

We have all felt kind of down at some point in our lives. So, in the quest of incorporating positivity into your life, you have to look at what the source is that makes you feel down or negative. Sort out your emotions and feels to pinpoint what it is that is actually making you feel that way. This can help you manage those feelings and eventually turn them into positives with consistent management.

Here are some tips you can use to help you when negative feelings start to come up:

1. **Expressing your feelings in appropriate ways -** Keeping feelings in that are causing stress, anxiety or sadness can actually make you feel worse both emotionally and physically. It is OK to tell someone that there is something bothering you. However, if you cannot come to terms with the feelings then you need perhaps someone on a more professional level to help you which is fine too. The main thing is you get the help and support you need to become positive in your life for you.

2. **Try and Live a Balanced Life -** Try not to obsess about those things that cause the negative feelings in the first place. For example if it's a work issue, leave it at work when you come home. This does not mean to pretend to be happy when you are not; what it means is to deal with the source of the negative feelings so they are not overwhelming your sense of self and positivity in your life. It's important to address negative feelings but to also keep track of the positive ones as well. Emphasize all those good things you got going while the negative feelings creep in to balance them out. If you have to write them down to keep track of them then do so. Keeping a positive journal to look at when you feel negative is very helpful. Write in it all the things that make you feel both happy and peaceful so when you need to be reminded you can read them. . Research has shown that a positive outlook gives way to a better quality of life as well as a health boost. People live longer when they are in a positive mindset. Being positive may also mean that you will need to let go of those things that overwhelm and stress you out in your life also. It's also important to make time for those things you enjoy.

3. **Develop Resilience** - Learning to bounce back is very important to have in the positivity equation. It has been found that people who have resilience can cope with life's stresses and problems better than those that don't. They tend to succeed where others can't despite the odds. Learning inner strength and becoming resilient can be learned by incorporating different strategies to help. Keeping a positive attitude even in conflict, accepting change and keeping things in perspective all are strategies in helping to develop resilience.

4. **Calm Your Body and Mind** - When our emotions and bodies are in harmony we tend to be positive then. It's important to do things to maintain the body and mind's state of balance. Relaxation techniques, such as meditation, or guided thoughts help in this regard. Exercising like Yoga or Ti Chi is also good for your mind and body. Whatever it takes for you, in this regard to help calm and keep you balanced, is positive. Stretching and Deep Breathing is also good.

Basically, to be positive means to take care of yourself. Eating healthy, getting enough sleep and rest, exercise and doing things you enjoy all help to curtail negativity.

The health benefits of being positive include:

1. Increasing your life span

2. Lower rate of depression

3. Lower rate of distress

4. Greater resistance to things like colds

5. Better psychological and physical well being

6. Reduce risk of death from cardiovascular disease

7. Better coping skills during hardships and times of stress

Don't forget laughter and humor; it goes a long way on the positivity scale. Besides keeping you young, it also helps with all the health benefits above.

CHAPTER 7

Positivity and Creative Visualization

Creative visualization is a tool that is used to stimulate one's imagination to making dreams come true. Using creative visualization in the right way can help us improve our lives for the better and attract to us what we want. It is a power that can alter our present environment and circumstances and actually cause events to happen, attract money, possessions, work, people and love into our lives.

Creative visualization is a tool that harnesses the power of the mind to succeed in getting what you want out of your life.

Using creative visualization by seeing in what we want helps us to attract it in our lives. It is a process that is similar to daydreaming. Why a lot of people even do every day without even knowing what it is they are doing. Successful people do this both consciously and unconsciously to achieve what they want all the time. They attract success by visualization that they have achieved their goals already.

You may say well I think all the time so how and why does this work anyway. It is a fact that thoughts are powerful things in and of themselves. So how it works is that our thoughts are accepted on a subconscious level in our minds which changes our mindsets. When one changes their mindset it also changes habits and outlooks as well. It's the changes that bring us into new situations and guide us to what we want.

Thoughts are creative energy that the brain creates. They can travel from person to person both consciously when we share our thoughts and unconsciously to those who are in tuned to the power of thought.

It is through this process where thoughts are transferred that when the right people pick up on our thoughts help us to manifest what we want.   The other part of the equation is the power of the Universe. This omnipotent power that we are part of is a universal life force of energy which also creates. When we think we are part of the universal process of creation. And the more well thought out the thought is; the more you repeat the same thought and define it the better it is for the universal power to carry that thought into the Universe for manifestation.

Thoughts are energy. They are energy created from our minds. Thoughts can change the balance of energy around us. This includes the energy in our environments. If you notice many times people think the same things over and over and thus recreate the same situations in their lives as a result. We can see what is going to happen in our minds eye as a result of what we think will happen to us based on our thoughts. It's this very factor where we can change the outcome to the movie we play in our heads with us as the stars of the film. So in essence when we change our thoughts and images that we manifest from our minds we change our state of reality also.

Since it is our thoughts that shape our state of being in our worlds this is what we change when we use creative visualization to change our realities. It's not magic or witchcraft it's the power of positive thought to manifest positive energy.

With creative visualization we dream realistic dreams and change them to what we want in our lives for the better. For instance if you live in a little cramped apartment; why not dream for a bigger home and money to buy it with. Change your thoughts; see yourself in that bigger apartment and home feel yourself living in it. Visualize and believe that you are living in a bigger apartment. This helps overcome the idea of limited thinking. It is limited thinking that keeps us from getting what we want in life. The more open minded we are the more possibilities to manifest what we want there are.

Creative visualization is not a quick magical fix. It's an approach to changing a state of mind and being. Sometimes you may actually see quick fast results and other times it takes work and longer. That is how life is.

Here are some guidelines to approach creative visualization with:

1. Define Your Goal

2. Think, meditate and listen to your intuition to ascertain that you really desire to attain this goal.

3. Ascertain that only good will result from your visualization, for you and for others.

4. Sit alone in a quiet place, where you will not be disturbed.

5. Relax your body.

6. Breathe rhythmically and deeply several times.

7. Visualize a clear and detailed mental image of what you desire to get or accomplish.

8. Use in your imagination all the five senses of sight, hearing, touch, smell and taste.

9. Add desire and feelings into what your mental image.

10. Visualize at least twice a day, about 10 minutes each time.

11. Persevere with your visualization, day after day, with, patience, hope and faith.

12. Stay positive, thinking positive thoughts, feeling positive feelings and using positive words.

13. During the day, when negative thoughts and doubts arise, replace them with positive thoughts. As each negative thought enters your mind, immediately substitute it with a positive thought.

14. Keep an open mind, so that you recognize opportunities and take advantage of them.

15. After concluding your visualization session, say attentively and earnestly, "Let everything happen in a harmonious and favorable way for all involved".

Please do not use the power of creative imagination for anything other than good for yourself or others. Keep in mind we manifest Karma by what we do in kind. Never try to use it to get something that belongs to others or hurt others. Make sure that what you are creating is good for all involved, and cause no harm to your environment.

Although manifestation of your will can happen fast most of the times it is a gradual occurrence where one thing leads to another naturally. For example if you wish for money; don't expect it to fall from the sky or by winning the Mega Millions. It may come from a new and better job, an opportunity or things of that nature. It is recommended that you approach creative visualization as mental work; with a positive attitude, earnestness and faith, but at the same time with some detachment, and regarding it as a sort of game or play. This attitude will prevent inner tension and disappointment, if things don't happen as expected.

Also after you have done your visualizing session let go what you visualized and give it in faith to the Universe. In other words, visualize several times a day for several minutes, and then forget for the rest of the day what you have visualized. By realizing the mental image, you free your conscious mind to become aware of the prompting of the subconscious mind. You make it possible for the subconscious mind to bring important information to your conscious mind. This action makes you become more aware of opportunities that pop up, and let the subconscious mind motivate you to take action, instead of just waiting for things to happen.

CHAPTER 8

Staying Positive Under Adversity

The hardest challenge in positivity is to remain positive when we are faced with adversity. The true test of being positive is the solutions we find to overcome the adversity. Staying positive in troubled times can take a life time to learn but it can be done.

The main thing is that when we are facing a problem that we get to the source of what is making the negativity it to try and put an end to it so we can endure on. Negative factors can really take a toll on everything we do. It sets in your mind that you cannot succeed or overcome your problems. Negativity instills in us that there is no solution to a bad situation so we just have to wallow in it and accept it. If you have trouble staying positive during a difficult time then it is suggested you write the problem down and research ways to alleviate the problem or problems you are experiencing. You may come to find others have the same problems you do when you research and you are not alone.

Being positive is one of the best traits a person can have. It keeps them proactive to succeed in their lives despite the odds against them. It activates your inner strength and allows you to remain in control of even the worst of situations. Staying positive in hard times is also a sign of maturity. It takes a mature person to stay positive when they are bombarded by negativity and problems.

Science has shown a correlation between the brain; a person's positive attitude and their body's response. Being positive can help an ailing body fight diseases better (eg., people who go into remission from cancer) and mentally to take on the challenges. Even if you fail or don't get the results you want it has been shown that it's easier to recover or continue on in a positive frame of mind. For example if you don't get a job you applied for you want fall apart you except it and keep looking until you do eventually find one.

Here are some tips to use to stay positive under adverse conditions:

1.Never Give Up - By not giving up, even under the hardest conditions, you go that little extra further to try and succeed. You find deep within that tiny bit of strength that's inside where you thought it was all gone.

2. Use Role Models to Keep You Inspired - When you find other people who have gone through what you are going through and have rose above it you can use their story to keep you inspired to not give up and remain positive as they did. It doesn't matter if the person is famous or not

3. Surround Yourself With Positive Influences - Friends and family can be a source of both comfort and support when you are going through rough times. If someone doesn't give you positive reinforcement in times of trouble then leave them alone. You don't need anyone or anything to tear you down when you are fighting for your life to be better.

4. Try not to wallow in feeling bad even if you are suffering This does not mean that you cannot mourn the loss of a loved one or grieve about it, but don't let it get to the point that it consumes you and prevents you from getting back to a positive point in your life again. If you have suffered a loss say to yourself "How can I value my life more?" " How can I make the most of my life now; even with the loss" and you also need to address the fact " Do you make the most of the relationships that you do have even though you are experiencing loss?" "Do you nurture and value your current relationships?" If you say no to any of those questions then you need to adjust your mindset and behavior to a yes.

.

5.   Divert Your Mind With Something Positive - When you feel negativity setting in do something positive to counteract it. Take a class and do that thing you never got around to doing. Read or meditate. Do whatever you need to keep yourself up in a positive frame of mind.

6.   Do Things to Keep Calm -Tension breeds negativity and adversity. If you have to, like number 5 says, meditate, listen to music, do Yoga, get a message, pamper yourself within your means, take a warm bath whatever it takes. And, keep reminding yourself that there is light at the end of the tunnel.

7.   Even If You Cannot Find A Job - Even if you aren't working it's recommended that you go outside everyday even just to take a walk and breathe fresh air. Learn to appreciate the simple things around you. Realize how blessed you are to be able to see, walk and experience life despite the setbacks it brings.

8.   Count Your Blessings - You may not have a lot materially but sometimes we are blessed with the little things we do have. Appreciation goes a long way.

9.   Exercise - It helps keep your body and mind strong. Even if you don't have money you will still feel like a million bucks.

10.   Surround yourself with people who are goal driven - It's important to surround yourself with positive people who are focused on achieving their goals in their lives as a motivating factor for you. Do not waste time with people who constantly complain or put your dreams down; including your plans for your future.

11.   Be persistent - If something didn't work the first time; don't give up. Try it again. Also look at ways to improve on the idea to make it work the next time.

12.   If you have a loved one in your life - Hug them and tell them you love them at least 2 times a day. This includes your children.

The best way to deal with adversity is to stay focused and organized to achieve your goals in spite of the difficulties. This is where the saying "keep your eye on the prize" can have some meaning. Devise a plan to attack the adverse conditions in a positive fashion and stick to it. Also take things as they come one day at a time. This way you don't put unrealistic expectations on yourself as you fight your way through the adversities and keeping a positive perspective while you do.

CHAPTER 9

The Power of Affirmations

Affirmations are positive statements we make and repeat to impress in our subconscious minds in order to affect a change. It is repeated in order to trigger the subconscious towards positive action. For affirmations to work they have to be repeated frequently. A practical example of affirmations and how they work is ... let's say you were in a race and you had to run 15 yards. Well by the 5th yard you start to feel tired but you keep saying to yourself "I can do this, I am going to finish" and you do! That is an example of how your mind propels you on to the end of the race.

What happens is that most of the time we repeat negative affirmations all the time. We say "I can't do that; that's impossible". As a result we have negativity and undesirable results in our lives. This is the power of the word. It can build or it can destroy. It's up to us how we use them. If we use them in a negative way or for negative intent that's just what it brings us. Many times we may repeat negative statements without even being conscious of it. If you tell yourself you can't do something over and over again you will fail. You are programming yourself to do so. The subconscious accepts anything we say negative or positive as truth. So if you understand this, then why not stay positive?

Affirmations function in the mind very much like programming a computer does. They work the same way creative visualization

(as discussed in earlier chapters) does. By repetition of a word or phrase you are focusing your aim, creating mental images that correspond in the conscious mind to the words or phrases.   This in turn affects the unconscious mind. We "think" with our conscious minds first and then the subconscious takes over. By consciously using affirmations you are reprogramming your subconscious. This is the key to reshaping your external life and conditions for the better.

Sometimes we see results quickly, sometimes we don't. It depends on your goal. Some things, with quick re-programming, we can see immediately, some take time. Also keep in mind if you are positive only when you say the affirmations and then go back to negative mindsets then you are neutralizing your affirmations. You have to think positive to have positive results. When you do affirmations it's important to say short phrases instead of long ones. In this way it is easier to remember. Repeat the phrases at any time; when you are on the bus, walking anywhere. Do not use them when you are driving or crossing the street. You have to use safety sense. It is suggested to repeat them for 5 to 10 minute sessions; several times a day. You must be in a physically and emotionally relaxed state; tension-free.

When you say the statements say them with conviction. Use only positive wording to describe what you want. For example if you want to loose weight don't say " I am Fat" say " I am getting slimmer" or " I am reaching my ideal weight". The second affirmations invoke positive images. Also affirm in the present tense not the future. For example if you say "I will be rich one day" that means you are not going to attain it in the immediate now. In cases like this, it is more effective to say "I am rich now". By stating what you want to be true in your life now the subconscious will work to make it happen in the conscious.

Here are some samples of positive affirmations:

- I am happy and healthy

- Wealth is pouring into my life

- I am sailing on the river of wealth (can use river of anything you want)

- I get wealthier every day

- My body is healthy and functioning in a very good way

- I have a lot of energy

- I study and comprehend fast

- My mind is calm

- I am calm and relaxed in every situation

- My thoughts are under my control

- I radiate love and happiness

- I am surrounded by love

- I have the perfect job for me

- I am living in the house of my dreams

- I have good and loving relationships with my husband/wife

- I have a wonderful and satisfying job

- I have the means to travel abroad whenever I want to

- I am successful in whatever I do

- Everything is getting better every day

CHAPTER 10

Meditation and Positivity

Meditation is another tool that is used for incorporating a positive mind state in ourselves. It can relax the body and free the mind from nagging thoughts and worries that are hard to get rid of. What meditation does is to quiet the chatter in the mind and also help you attain inner peace. These two things alone help create our own personal harmony within ourselves.   Although many religions incorporate some form of meditation, it is not a prerequisite to meditate. Anyone can meditate, it is non denominational. What it does do with consistent practice is open ourselves up to higher spirituality and for some enlightenment. There is no right or wrong way to meditate. There many techniques used to practice meditation. To experience the benefits of meditation it is recommended to meditate at least once a day; ideally twice. If you are new to meditation it is suggested you start with 10 minute sessions and then increase as you become better at it.

Basically there are two types of meditation. One kind requires focusing on a certain activity in conjunction with the meditating such as breathing. The other is to concentrate on a concrete image, object, word, thought or quality of character.   The goal when you meditate is to merge with your inner self as inner silence. This happens after you master the first type of meditating.

Here are some tips to help you meditate and get the most of your meditation sessions:

1. It is important to meditate every day.

2. Keep up a positive attitude.

3. Do not meditate when you are tired.

4. Meditate in a place where you can be alone and undisturbed.

5. Sit in a comfortable position with your spine erect. You can sit on the floor, on a cushion or even a chair.

6. Relax your body.

7. Take a few slow deep breaths.

8. To help increase your relaxation, focus on a pleasant memory for a few moments or a mental image that makes you feel calm.

9. Think for a few moments of the benefits of meditation; how it strengthens your focus, calms your mind down, eases stress and tension, etc.

10. Start meditating calmly, yet with focused attention. The more focused the attention is the easier it is to ignore thoughts and other distractions.

11. Keep calm both mentally and physically, and do not tense your body.

12. Patience, perseverance and self-discipline should be always cultivated.

13. 10 minutes are quite enough for a beginner.

Here are a couple of meditation techniques that you can use as one of your techniques to become positive in your life:

1. **Focus your attention on your incoming and outgoing breath.**
   For a few minutes, focus your attention on your breath. Breathe normally, while focusing on the act of breathing in and breathing out. Be careful not to strain your breath and your body.

2. **Focusing on an inspiring quote.**
   Choose an inspiring quote from any spiritual teacher, and repeat it in your mind, trying to find its deep meaning, beyond the written words.

CHAPTER 11

CONCLUSION: Achieving Your Dreams and Goals

The main purpose to incorporate positivity in our life is to achieve our dreams and goals. There are several factors one has to use in order to make their dreams reality. Dreams and goals are achieved because of several factors. The success of achieving what you want depends overall on the following things:

1. You should have a specific goal.

2. You have to be sure that you really want to achieve your goal.

3. You need to have a clear mental image of your goal.

4. You need a strong desire.

5. You need to disregard and reject doubts and thoughts about failure.

6. Show confidence and faith and persevere until you gain success.

The things above sound simple enough, but few really apply those ideas above in getting what they want. You don't need physical work to get what you want. What you do need is power of the mind in a constant positive state which is the law of positivity to achieve what you want.

It's about consciously changing your state of mind which in turn changes your state of being. Visualizations, affirmations and even meditation make up the mental work. It doesn't have to be a painful ordeal to incorporate a new positive mindset in your life. The human mind is geared to finding solutions in our lives to bring about what we want into manifestation. When you use tools like visualization and affirmations in your life, you are focusing and channeling your energy towards your goal. When you focus all your energy into a positive mindset, you are eliminating any negativity to creep in. Doubt is one of the worst killers of positivity there is. When you doubt yourself you do not succeed because you are saying you cannot achieve what you want for your life. Also, when you become positive, your intuition also starts to set in and look for opportunities towards positivity as well.

There are those people who also include using subliminal messaging into programming their minds in a positive manner. In this case they may listen to CDs that reinforce the idea of positivity in their subconscious while they sleep or meditate. There are many CDs that are available today on the market that does this. Many people use them because it requires no added effort to use them. The messages go straight to one's subconscious and work faster for that reason.

However, although using subliminal messages is fine, when you use affirmations and visualization you get added benefits that subliminal programming alone does not do. Affirmations, creative visualization and meditation helps you to develop inner strength, concentration, willpower and self-discipline. Those three tools help activate your inner power. Another benefit of affirmations and creative visualization is that you can use them anywhere and anytime. You need no external instruments just your mind.

Success is something that manifests in a person's life in different ways. Sometimes it may appear as a miracle and other times it's a subtle thing. It can be nothing more than an ordinary opportunity we have been waiting for that comes to being. Success may mean no more than a door opening, but it's up to you to see the door and go through it. Remember, we have big goals and then we have our daily goals.

People make mistakes when they think that big goals only mean things like being wealthy, having an expensive car, having a big house with a pool or building a business empire. Yes these are big goals, but a big goal can also be simple goals like spending time with one's loved ones, finding true love or even eating less.

Just remember, a big goal does not have to be materialistic to be big. It is a goal you set for yourself that is positive that is a big goal!

To Cuz

Roa Vineyard